T0164866

KISSING
the
GROUND

A Personal Journey overcoming life's
challenges using The Law of Attraction

NANCI STONE

BALBOA.
PRESS
A DIVISION OF HAY HOUSE

Copyright © 2014 Nanci Stone.

All rights reserved. No part of this book may be used or reproduced by any means, graphic, electronic, or mechanical, including photocopying, recording, taping or by any information storage retrieval system without the written permission of the publisher except in the case of brief quotations embodied in critical articles and reviews.

Balboa Press books may be ordered through booksellers or by contacting:

Balboa Press
A Division of Hay House
1663 Liberty Drive
Bloomington, IN 47403
www.balboapress.com
1 (877) 407-4847

Because of the dynamic nature of the Internet, any web addresses or links contained in this book may have changed since publication and may no longer be valid. The views expressed in this work are solely those of the author and do not necessarily reflect the views of the publisher, and the publisher hereby disclaims any responsibility for them.

The author of this book does not dispense medical advice or prescribe the use of any technique as a form of treatment for physical, emotional, or medical problems without the advice of a physician, either directly or indirectly. The intent of the author is only to offer information of a general nature to help you in your quest for emotional and spiritual well-being. In the event you use any of the information in this book for yourself, which is your constitutional right, the author and the publisher assume no responsibility for your actions.

Any people depicted in stock imagery provided by Thinkstock are models, and such images are being used for illustrative purposes only.
Certain stock imagery © Thinkstock.

Printed in the United States of America.

ISBN: 978-1-4525-2245-6 (sc)
ISBN: 978-1-4525-2246-3 (e)

Library of Congress Control Number: 2014916612

Balboa Press rev. date: 11/18/2014

Words do not teach. Your true knowledge comes from your own *life experience, and while you will be a constant gatherer of experience and knowledge, your life is not only about that, it is about fulfillment, satisfaction, and joy. Your life is about the continuing expression of who you truly are.*

Abraham-Hicks

Acknowledgment

I want to thank my sons, Christopher and Mark, who relived many of my past experiences for the purpose of writing this book. To Tami, who through her gentle spirit has loved and supported me. To my brother and sister for sharing their lives, even though we are on very different journeys. Especially to my sister, Susan, who I love with all my heart. Thank you to all of the people in this book. It is my hope that, on your own journey, you find love, peace and happiness.

I dedicate this to every one of us who is searching for the truth of who we are and believes they are worthy and loved enough to honor who they are.

The Emotional Scale

By Abraham-Hicks

1. JOY/KNOWLEDGE/EMPOWERMENT/FREEDOM/ LOVE/APPRECIATION
2. PASSION
3. ENTHUSIASM/EAGERNESS/HAPPINESS
4. POSITIVE EXPECTATION/BELIEF
5. OPTIMISM
6. HOPEFULNESS
7. CONTENTMENT
8. BOREDOM
9. PESSIMISM
10. FRUSTRATION/IRRITATION/IMPATIENCE
11. FEELING OVERWHELMED
12. DISAPPOINTMENT
13. DOUBT
14. WORRY
15. BLAME
16. DISCOURAGEMENT
17. ANGER
18. REVENGE

19. HATRED/RAGE
20. JEALOUSY
21. INSECURITY/GUILT/UNWORTHINESS
22. FEAR/GRIEF/DEPRESSION/DISPAIR/
    POWERLESSNESS

The concept behind the "Emotional Scale" is simple, really. By acknowledging how I'm feeling, I can choose to feel better. For example, the higher the number, the higher your vibration. If you start the day feeling worried (#14 on the scale), aim for a higher vibration. For instance, you might think of something that you're disappointed about because Disappointed is two steps up from being worried. From there, you work up the scale, and aim to be somewhere between a #1 and a #3 throughout most of the day. You then *appreciate* your way up the scale until you get there. The "Emotional Scale" is a tool I personally use every day.

Foreword

As I look back on the past year, I can see how much I've grown. It's because of this growth that I have so much to share with you. Even though I started this book over two years ago, I was recently inspired by a director named Nina Davenport to finish. Nina filmed a documentary about her life and her own emotional journey. During the two years she filmed, Nina became a single mother and had her share of ups and downs.

Nina's journey, all the highs and lows of her life, stirred something deep inside me. There wasn't any one thing that I connected with, but I identified with the struggles of her everyday life. As I watched, I wanted to know more and more, and I watched her documentary in its entirety. Finally I realized why I was so invested in her story...... It wasn't the highs and lows she experienced that kept me glued to the screen, it was how she handled those highs and lows that captivated me the most. I may not know Nina, but that didn't stop me from taking a keen interest in her story. I asked myself "Why? What's so interesting and what did I take away from watching it?"

The answers to those questions are what inspired me to write this book. Her story is about choices and experiences, and these are things we're all faced with in our daily lives. If I could be so inspired by her story, maybe others could be inspired by reading my book.

Introduction

When I sat down to write this book, I hoped it would speak to someone who was seeking their own truth of who they were. The creation of this book, to my surprise, has brought even more gifts. It has reminded me there is always hope, and we are never really alone. It has given me closure through the beautiful art of forgiving. It also reminded me, from the teachings of Abraham-Hicks, "Know you never get it wrong because there is no right or wrong: and know you will never get it all done."

Most of the names of the people in this story have been changed. It is not my intent to embarrass anyone.

The dark days of my youth and early adulthood have passed. The confusion has melted away. Forgiveness was the key. Now, I am in a great place in my life, eager to grow more and I'm eager to share. I wake up every morning with that excited feeling in the pit of my stomach for the unfolding of the day. I look forward to the great things to unfold in my life, and I continue to seek to uncover the meaning of the challenges. I no longer live in fear, and have let go of the guilt and shame of the past.

Writing this book has brought the healing of the past which has set me free – free to allow loving relationships to begin and free to trust in myself and others. It's true that I use the "Emotional Scale" every single day, just as I stated at the beginning of this book. It is a reminder that no matter what I am feeling, I have the choice to feel better.

The experiences I write about are real and the referenced material is a part of what I have used to grow as a person. I have had many mentors: people that I admire, authors of books, seminar hosts, and friends. Our mentors in life make it possible for us to grow.

It is my hope that you use this book to inspire the next step in your spiritual journey. Everything I have experienced and what I have come to know is not only for me, but for you as well. It wasn't easy to share some of my experiences, but I hope my experiences give you the inspiration to get ready and start in your own healing. If you are asking yourself IF you are ready, let me share one thing that I do know. If you are reading this book, then you ARE ready and in a place of finding out who you are.

It is when we are in alignment with who we are, and true to ourselves, that we can share and create loving relationships, wonderful careers, and understand what our life purpose is. It is a place where we stop controlling other peoples lives, love unconditionally and most importantly, we accept those people for who they are. That's our journey, and this what I hope for you.

Chapter 1

My Relationship With My Father

This chapter is about my early years growing up. It was also the hardest chapter to write, bringing me healing and closure.

My memories from childhood are scattered and mostly unpleasant. It's now interesting for me to realize that my feelings and emotions were simply my perception at the time. In reality, there's no way I can verify if either parent felt the way I perceived them to feel about me. The memories of my father are mostly sad, and prior to my father's passing, most of my memories were blocked. With both my parents deceased, I'll never know how they really felt about me. It doesn't matter the intention of others, it only matters the perception one perceives.

Like many children, I was also seeking my parent's approval, especially my father's. I adored my father, and he was well-liked by everyone who knew him. I thought he was the most wonderful person in the world. He was tall, handsome, and I was always told how much I looked like him. I was proud of my father, and naturally, I wanted him to be proud of me. Sadly, even though I thought the world of my father, I never felt like he loved me. I always felt he loved my brother and sister more because I wasn't good enough to earn his love.

I was the oldest of three. My father always wanted his first child to be a boy, and obviously that didn't happen because he got me, a daughter, instead. A year later, my brother Mark was born. As his only son, my father preferred spending time with Mark, or as we called him, "The Begotten." I often wondered if Mark had been first, would that have made a difference to how my father felt about me? Eight years later, my little sister was born, and she was absolutely adored by all. Not only was she adored by my parents, I thought she was a gift for my life. She was my real life doll, and I attended to her care all the time. Susan was the "surprise" baby, and because of this, she brought so much love, laughter and happiness to our family.

I always felt I was in trouble for something, and it seemed my father was almost always angry with me. He'd come home from work, and I'd be excited to see him, but my excitement would quickly wane when he appeared irritated. His anger would be directed toward me. I never understood what I did to irritate him, nor can I remember any one thing that I had done to deserve the frequent punishments.

It felt like he didn't love me, yet I always aimed for my father's acceptance. I don't remember working as hard for my mother, but then again, my father was our primary parent. Not that mom didn't discipline us, she did. However, it was my father who made the decisions and executed the discipline, and because of that, it was his approval and acceptance I wanted.

I never got it. Or at least, in my perception, I felt like I hadn't. Up until the day he died, I never felt I had his love or acceptance.

I often look back and wonder *what did I do wrong?* At the age of 12 years old, what could I have done that caused my own father to reject me? Now the question is *did I ever do anything wrong at all?*

I was punished with a belt, and I was punished frequently. Yet, I only vaguely remember my brother and sister ever being disciplined. Even as he was weak and dying, he could always muster up a reason to be angry at me for something. Only one example I can remember, although there were several instances, I walked home from school with a friend who lived several blocks away. I remember I stopped at her house for a drink of water before continuing my walk home which made me late in my arrival home. My father was livid. He was yelling so loud that he started coughing, spitting up blood. It was at that exact moment that no matter what anyone said, I knew my father didn't love me, and my very presence was irritating to him. My father passed away less than a month later, and I carried the guilt and felt responsible for the timing of his passing. I thought then, and believed my entire life, that if I had not made him so angry, he would have lived longer.

My father always made a great production out of my punishments. Whenever I'd get into trouble, my father would order me to walk to his closet and pick out a belt. My mother would be sitting on the couch, crying, and the hallway to his bedroom seemed so very long. Whenever I'd reach the bedroom, I'd stand in front of his closet, looking at all the belts hanging. Some were brown, some were black. Some had fancy buckles, others did not. But what really mattered, in that moment, was their width. If I stood there too long, I'd hear my father's footsteps echoing down the hallway. I'd quickly grab the thickest belt I could find. As a child, I experienced enough spankings to know thinner belts stung twice as much as thicker ones. To this day, I can remember the nausea that would overcome me. The anticipation of each lash would make my body hurt, and

I'd close my eyes, pretend I was somewhere else. I'd pretend that I was a princess in a faraway land... A land where everyone loved me.

The night I found out that my father had cancer, I heard my parents talking in a low voice, almost a whisper. It was the weeping that caught my attention, however. My mom was sitting in my father's lap, both crying. They were holding on to each other, and in that moment, I realized my life was going to change dramatically. No one had told me my father was dying, but in that moment, I knew.

We were told he only had three months to live, but my father was a fighter. He fought for his life for just under a year. As his illness progressed, my father seemed to age before my very eyes. Despite his young age of thirty-six, by the time he died, his hair was completely gray. The only treatment were the pain pills to keep him as comfortable as possible, there was no cure, nothing to give us hope for a better outcome. My father was 6'5", and before cancer, he was every bit of 240 pounds. During his last few months, I watched him dissolve down to a frail 90 pounds right before my eyes. Every day, I would watch my mother feed my father, and I'd sometimes help feed him as well. On these rare occasions, I felt so proud to be able to help and secretly wondered if my father appreciated it. The day he passed away, my mother kept me home from school to care for my sister. On that cold January 3rd morning, my father had told my mother he was ready to die. He asked to go to the hospital because he didn't want to die at home.

At around 10:30 am, I took my sister to the corner store. My mom had insisted I take her for a walk, and it wasn't until later that I found out the ambulance was picking my father up at that time. My mother didn't want my sister and I to be there. As I stood on the corner, waiting for the green light to cross the street, a funeral procession passed in front of me. Police on motorcycles stopped traffic, and we had to wait for the procession to pass by before we could cross the street. My father passed away at 8:35 that evening, and to this day, I feel that the funeral procession was a sign of what was to come. For years afterward, I would avoid letting them pass in front of me, believing that if I did, it was a sign that my mother, brother, or sister would die soon.

Despite my childhood, my father's death was still very traumatic for me. For me, his passing meant that I would never get his approval. More importantly, it meant I would never have the chance to earn his love.

Chapter 2

Life After My Father

The passing of my father was devastating not only to us, but to the rest of his family as well. His parents lived in Arkansas, but they visited frequently those last few months, as did his brother and sister-in-law. My mother's family visited frequently those last months. Being that her family was very large, eight brothers and sisters with their own families as well, it seemed like there was always people around.

On the day of the funeral, I walked around the house angry that all these people were around. I wanted to scream, "Why are you here? Leave us alone!" Aunts, uncles, and cousins were hugging each other and crying, and I felt so much anger. I wanted to ask them, "What does this have to do with you?" It has to do with my mother, brother, sister and I. When my grandmother hugged one of my cousins, I thought to myself: *Why are you hugging her? I just lost my father. She didn't lose her father.* They were intrusive, and I never got the feeling that they were there for us. Even as I wanted them to leave, there was still fear in the back of my mind. I kept thinking, *What's going to happen to us?*

Two weeks prior to this, it had been Christmas. It obviously wasn't a good Christmas, but it wasn't bad either. There was a knock on the door, and since my father was bed-ridden at this point, my mother answered it. A stranger was standing in the doorway, arms full of presents and a big smile spread across her face. "Merry Christmas!" she said, and my mother invited her in. Later on, I found out that she was from our church. While she was joyful and happy, I just wanted her to leave. I felt she was intruding, and I had no interest in her presents.

But regardless, the presents were put under the tree, and my father was brought out into the living room. Unlike me, my brother and sister were very excited about the presents, and they started opening them right away. These gifts weren't from my parents, nor were they from family. They were from a strange woman at church, and I wanted nothing to do with them. My mother insisted, and I didn't want to anger my father, so I reluctantly opened those addressed to "oldest child."

I opened a lot of presents, but only one stood out to me. A watch. I thought it was the most beautiful, grown-up watch I'd ever seen. Despite admiring its beauty, I never wore that watch. In fact, I have no idea what happened to it. It reminded me of my dying father and all the pain I was going through at that time. Less than two weeks after Christmas, my father passed away. I entered into a completely new stage of anger at this point. I wanted to be alone with my family - and by that, I meant my mother, brother, and sister. I didn't want people to stop by, and I didn't want to eat food made by extended family or friends. I remember thinking that we'd be just fine, that we didn't need them. I'm not sure what it is about death that tears a family apart, but people lose sight of what really matters after a loved one passes away. A couple of months after my dad passed, my mother found herself in the midst of several battles with both her own family and my father's. My paternal grandparents, aunt, and uncle tried to get custody of us, claiming that my mother wasn't fit to care for us since she hadn't worked in years. After they failed to get custody, my mother's family decided it was their turn to cause my mother trouble. First, they came to her for a loan, assuming she had life insurance money from my father. When she insisted that she had no such money, as there was no life insurance, they didn't believe her. Then, just like my father's family, they also tried to take us from my mother.

Before my father passed away in January, they'd already secured a vacation house for our annual summer trip to Seal Beach. My mother believed it was important for us to go even after everything we'd been through. However, a couple days prior to our vacation, our family car died and my mom took it to the local Ford dealership. A car salesman named Bud arranged for a car rental so that we could still take our family vacation.

Chapter 3

My Stepfather

The first week at the beach house was wonderful. I enjoyed spending time with just my mother, brother and sister. The house was a two-story home with a patio with rattan furniture where we would sit outside every morning and evening watching the people walk by. Only sidewalk and the beautiful white sand separated us from the ocean. We met other vacationers and played on the beach all day, and for the first time in my life, I felt happiness.

A week into our vacation, there was a knock on our front door. My mother answered it and invited in a man I didn't know who carried a bag of groceries. She introduced him to us as Bud, the salesman who loaned her the car so we could still go on vacation. They went into the kitchen, and I just stood there for a moment, shocked at what just happened. My mom hadn't mentioned she was expecting anyone, and I felt like he was intruding on our family vacation. I was so angry that he was there. Him and my mom carried on like this was normal, talking and laughing while Bud grilled some steaks. Unlike me, my brother was excited and attempted to get Bud's attention.

After dinner, Bud asked me to take my sister and brother to the corner store for ice cream. Our eyes met and we held each other's stare as I refused to take the money from him. I believe that was the moment Bud realized I'd never accept him, and I realized he'd make my life hell if I crossed him. At my mother's insistence, I took the money and walked to the store. Secretly, I hoped he'd be gone when we got back, but upon our return, Bud was still there. He was acting weird, however, and it wasn't until later I found out he was drunk. I'd never witnessed my own parents drunk before. If they drank, it was at social gatherings, not around us kids. Little did I know at the time, this would become a common occurrence in my life.

I took my sister upstairs for the rest of the evening and while I can't remember specific details about the first night I met Bud, I know I wasn't very nice to him. I might have embarrassed my mother. I was not a happy girl, going through many different emotions and still grieving heavily. The next morning, I got up and took my sister downstairs for breakfast. I was stunned to find Bud lying on the living room floor and thought perhaps he'd died the night before. But when I heard my mom preparing breakfast in the kitchen like normal, I was very confused. She told me that Bud had passed out and to not worry about him. She wasn't concerned, and I just stood there, looking at this strange man sprawled out on the floor. I already didn't care for him and felt he was intruding, and there he was passed out on our floor. Whether I liked it or not, this man was part of my life now, and this was the beginning of a rather rocky and turbulent relationship between Bud and I.

At 13 years old, my relationship with my mother was already strained, and I was even more upset at her for bringing Bud into our life. My father hadn't even been dead a year, and while I was still grieving, trying to deal with my emotions, she brought another man into our lives. I wasn't ready.

Bud was my mother's first boyfriend after my father's death, and at the time, I didn't understand why she needed another man in her life. As I matured, I understood why she might seek the companionship. However, I treated Bud very badly, and I never gave him a chance to fill any voids in my life. Because of this, our relationship never improved. Looking back, I don't think he would have been able to fill the void in my life, but Bud wanted nothing more than for me to accept him. As time passed and I didn't open up to him, his resentment for me grew.

When Bud drank, he became verbally abusive. Only my brother was spared since he could do no wrong in my stepfather's eyes. Bud's son had been killed in a car accident, and he was the same age as my brother when he died. My stepfather saw my brother as a replacement for his own son, thus sparing him the abuse the rest of us suffered.

By the time I turned sixteen, however, the verbal abuse turned into him physically pushing us around when he was drunk. I was as tall as he was and my height intimidated him, so he had to be really drunk to try and push me around. He was a coward. I knew it, and he knew it too.

I was angry and felt betrayed by my own mother, and during those early years, I ran away several times. I constantly worried about my sister and mother at home, but I simply hated my life at home so much, I had to get away.

I'd always go to the same place, a place where I found solace and comfort. About a mile from my home was a stable where I kept my horse, Gypsy. I'd sleep in her stall, or sometimes sleep in an old trailer that was parked on the property. Either way, my mother always knew where to find me - everyone did, including the property owner and the other horse owners. I was the incorrigible girl who wouldn't mind her parents. I never told anyone about the abuse because I was ashamed.

I simply wished for a normal family and a normal life. At that time, it was rare for kids to be raised by only one of their parents. Even more rare were those who had a step-parent. I was the odd girl, the girl who lost her father. Everyone pitied me, and I knew it. I hated that feeling.

We lived in Orange, California. Unlike today where there are over 3 million people living there, in 1968, the city was rural. My father had bought a home located at the bottom of the foothills near the orange groves. It was my parent's dream home, and it was everything I had dreamed a home could be.

During my stepfather's abusive drinking spells, we'd often have to call the police. That never did much good, however, since Bud had grown up in Orange and had gone to school with many of the local police officers. When they'd get to the house, they usually just sent him to bed with a warning that if he didn't stop, they would have to take him to jail. Of course, we called the police often and they never once took him away. In those days, domestic violence wasn't taken as seriously as it is today. It was treated as a family problem, not something the police usually got involved in.

I was alone. I had no one to talk to, not even my mother. At one time, I could remember playing with cousins, enjoying family get-togethers. But they too disliked Bud, and once my mom brought him into our lives, my extended family distanced themselves from us.

When I was 16, Bud convinced my mother to move the family to Oregon. When my mother told us, my brother and I were very upset at leaving our home. Unfortunately, we had little say in the matter because my mom had already purchased a quaint general store/gas station in Bandon, Oregon. We left our 2-story, five bedroom dream home behind for an apartment and a couple hotel rooms. There was a small apartment attached to the store where my mother, sister and Bud lived. There was also a small, run-down motel on the property, housing four rooms. That's where my brother and I lived. Each room had a small living room, tiny kitchen, bedroom and bathroom. While I constantly killed mice, roaches, and the like, I enjoyed the isolation away from my family. This became my private area, my space, and I learned to love it.

I went into my sophomore year of high school in Bandon. There was only one red school building that housed all the grades from kindergarten to seniors in high school. I loved my school, and before long, I started enjoying my new life in Oregon. I loved working in the general store, pumping gas, and helping my mom. We owned several acres and I made plans to board a horse, but Bud refused to let me get one. Thankfully, I became friends with kids who lived on farms, and I enjoyed working with them, milking cows, and riding their horses. Right before school started, I met a young man named Bryan visiting his cousins in Bandon. The ironic part of this friendship was that he also lived in Orange, California. We felt this was a sign we were meant to be together forever. Instead of going back to California, he talked his parents into letting him stay in Bandon and attend high school there. Bryan and his cousins were the popular kids, the football players, and his family was very affluent in Bandon. Bryan and I were inseparable. I never had to ride the bus to school, he picked me up and dropped me off after school each day. Bryan and I went steady for that year.

Bryan was possessive, always wanting me to be with him, and he soon became jealous anytime I talked to other boys at school. I thought he was being silly and would tell him so. That following summer, my mother sent my brother, sister, and me to Arkansas to stay with our grandparents. We spent most of the summer there, but

Bryan kept insisting I come back early. When I didn't, he hitchhiked from Oregon to Arkansas. However, it took him weeks to get there, and by the time he got there, we'd already returned to Oregon. Bryan showed up to my Grandmother's home and was picked up by the local Sheriffs where he was promptly escorted back to Orange. However, once home, Bryan hitchhiked back to Oregon to be with me. There was a lot of drama, but in the end, Bryan was once again taken back to California.

And as it turned out, Bud's drinking got out of control that year, and he kept leaving my mother and returning to Orange. Since my mom was unable to handle the store herself, we returned to Orange and I finished out my high school education at El Modena High.

I stayed to myself my junior and senior year. I wasn't popular, and I simply got lost in the crowds of high school. My junior year, Bud lost his son in an accident. We all went to school together, and we all knew each other. The exact details of the accident were never figured out, but it was deemed an accident and the investigation ended.

Chapter 4

Fresh Start

After graduating high school, my mother co-signed for a small apartment for me and I moved out. Truthfully, I think this was a way for my mother to keep the peace with Bud who wanted me to move out. My best friend, Kathy, moved in with me against her parent's wishes, and for the first time, it felt like things were going to be okay. I found a full-time job working in security, and I enrolled in night classes. Originally, I majored in nursing, but the classes bored me. After my first year of college, I switched over to study criminology.

In 1973, very few females studied criminology. My roommate, Kathy, and I were the exception. Most of my college classes were with men, but the surrounding police departments were promoting the idea of hiring woman. Because of my past with Bud, I wanted nothing more than to become a police officer. I wanted to help the abused families like mine. Not only that, I loved criminology, and it fascinated me. I did very well in my classes, and I graduated with an Associates Degree in 1975.

It was in one of my college classes that I met Jack, a police officer from the Los Angeles Police Department. He was sixteen years my senior, and he impressed me with his stature and personality. Jack was taking college classes to earn his Associates in Criminology so he could earn a promotion.

During breaks, Jack and I would talk about class topics, and I found him very easy to talk to. After every class, we would walk in the parking lot and talk, and over time, our discussions became longer and more personal. The fact that he was already a police officer made me feel secure. The first time Jack kissed me in the parking lot, I was surprised, but also excited that he liked me. However, in my naivety, I failed to realize that my relationship with Jack was confined to seeing him at night school and on an occasional Saturday afternoon. I never gave our structured time much thought, but eventually Jack confessed that he was married and had two children.

By this time, I was completely in love with Jack, or so I thought. Like many married men, Jack promised that he was going to leave his wife so we could be together. Like many girls drawn in by a married man, I naively believed him. I wanted to believe him so badly because he was the first man that treated me like he cared.

But after coming out about his marriage, Jack's demeanor changed almost instantly. He became very jealous, questioning my every move. I made excuses for his behavior, taking blame for his jealousy, always believing I'd done something wrong. As time passed, Jack wouldn't allow me to go out with my friends, and soon they all drifted away. He even turned my best friend, Kathy, against me, and I against her. He told me that Kathy was sending him love letters, and he told Kathy that I didn't like living with her anymore. As a result of the drama, Kathy moved out and we didn't speak for many years.

In addition to controlling my social life, he also forbade me from seeing my family. On one occasion, my mother invited me to meet my sister and her at Disneyland to spend the day together. I hadn't seen them in awhile, so I met up with them and we had a great day. However, upon returning to my apartment, Jack was sitting in his car waiting for me. He was livid. We walked into my apartment, and I didn't even get the front door closed before he punched me in the face, sending me backwards into a bookcase. The bookcase came down on me along with everything that had been sitting on it. The television came crashing down, hitting the floor and breaking. I had a 410 shotgun that I had since I was 16, and he repeatedly hit me with. He was enraged, and I remember praying that someone would hear and call the police, even though Jack himself was a police officer.

After it was over with, he calmed down and begged me to forgive him, promising that it would never happen again. He always made the same promises after every incident. I was in denial and hid the abuse from everyone. Jack stalked me for months, waiting in the parking lot where I worked, where I lived, and he made sure I wasn't talking to anyone. I prayed that no one would say "hi" to me, or stop to chat because I was being watched. I took full responsibility for my abuse, telling myself that I needed to be better so as to not upset Jack. He loved me, and all I wanted was that love. In order to win his love, I wore what he wanted me to wear, I talked to people he allowed me to talk to. I walked around in an isolated hell of his control.

Looking back, the abuse I was receiving from Jack was obvious to everyone. Here I thought I was the master of concealment, but others around me noticed. I had to move three times because my neighbors would talk to Jack or me about the abuse, and Jack would make me move. All I felt was fear, and he threatened to kill me if I ever left him or if the abuse was ever reported because he would lose his job as a police officer. I simply had to pretend that everything was okay. I had no doubt that he would kill me.

Over the next year, the abuse continued, and I continued to live in denial until one chilling night. A night I thought was my last night alive. In order to make sure I didn't leave my apartment, Jack started taking my car to work. Every morning at 5:30 am, on his way to work, he would stop at my place, pick my car up, and leave his car parked at my apartment. He wanted to make sure I couldn't go anywhere or see anyone. On this particular evening, Jack showed up to my apartment to drop off my car. He was drunk. In his drunkenness, he accused me of sneaking around and cheating on him. From there, he started hitting me again and again, and like so many times before, I prayed that someone in the apartment would call the police. I couldn't help but think how ludicrous this was. Here I was, running a mental tally of everything I'd done to try and please this man, and none of his accusations were true. I was, in a sense, his prisoner. There was no way I could sneak around. Jack bought me the clothes he wanted me to wear, and the food for me to eat. During the year, I lost a lot of weight. He also bought me a puppy and a bird to keep me company while he was away, but I couldn't visit with neighbors or family unless he approved.

On this particular night, in his jealous rage, he pulled his gun from the holster and pointed it at my head. He told me he was going to kill me. He grabbed me by the hair, and I felt the coldness and pressure of the barrel against my right temple. After the initial bout of fear, I felt a different emotion. Instead of being scared, I felt at peace. I honestly felt that dying was my only way out. I was calm knowing I was going to die, and part of me wanted to. I wanted to be released from the hell that I was living in. He didn't shoot, obviously. Instead, he raged on for hours, threatening to pull the trigger at any time, but that time never came. To this day, I often wonder *what saved me?*

My only explanation is that I wasn't alone that night. The calming and peacefulness that settled around me was beautiful, and I remember thinking how wonderful it would be to die. Something was protecting me, however. Was it God? Angels? Spiritual Guides? Or maybe, all of these. Whatever it was, I know that I wasn't alone that night, and something or someone was watching over me to make sure I survived the night. Jack eventually calmed down and left my apartment after I promised I wouldn't leave. The next morning, as usual, Jack showed up and took my car to work as if nothing had happened the night before. However, the moment he left, I found the inner strength to finally reach out for help. I called my brother and asked him to pick me up. I was terrified not only for myself, but for my brother as well. I knew if Jack caught us, he'd kill us both. But it was something I had to do. My brother showed up and took me to my mother's home. My mom contacted the local police and explained the situation. Finally, I felt somewhat safe.

We had arranged for police officers to stand by, and at one point, Jack had to return my car. When he came by my mother's house, he insisted on taking my puppy, likely knowing it would hurt me. My mother insisted I turn the dog over to him. As I handed the puppy over to Jack, in a very low, controlled voice, he threatened to kill me.

It wasn't until years later that I was introduced to the concept of a person's *energy* and *vibration*, which I explain in more detail later in the book. I came to understand the Laws of Attraction and the concept that *like attracts like.* I would later realize that by changing my vibration, I could stop attracting the abuse into my life. This knowledge didn't come easily for me. It took many years, and another horrendous relationship before I finally stopped attracting the abuse.

Chapter 5

New Beginnings

I may have left the abuse of Jack behind, but I was right back in the dysfunctional situation with Bud. While I felt somewhat safe at my mother's home, living with Bud again was difficult for me to deal with. Bud's drinking was more frequent, and because I was so much more independent, I became a target for his drunken outrages. It seemed like Bud was always drunk, and he could never keep a job.

Clearly my mother was unhappy, but she still kept Bud around. In her defense, she had started back to college and became involved in different causes which kept my mom away a lot. I felt compelled to stay close for my sister who was only 11 years old. My brother joined the Air Force and was gone. In his drunken stupors, Bud often tried to push my mother down the stairs. I worried that one day he'd finally succeed, but I felt powerless to help. Living at home was a daily reminder of abuse I'd experience with Jack.

Within a year, I finally moved to an apartment not far from my mother. It was far enough away from the daily abuse for me to escape, but close enough that I could still protect my mom and sister if need be. At this point, I was emotionally drained. Yet, somehow, I found the strength to move forward. I felt free and worked toward claiming my life back. I returned to college to finish my degree. I was only twenty-one years old when I finished college, but it felt like I'd already lived an entire lifetime. After graduating, I started to apply to the police departments in my area, all the while looking over my shoulder for Jack. Jack's last words to me were etched into my brain. Almost a year later, with renewed confidence, I started working for a security company as a scheduler and dispatcher. That's where I met Craig. Craig was my best friend as well as my companion. We didn't date immediately, but we became good friends and that developed into something more. Craig and I were both tired of Southern California, so we decided to move to Washington where we started a construction company. I was excited about getting far, far away from Orange.

Craig and I were together for almost seven years. We both worked hard. I worked as a model and did odd jobs to keep money coming in, while Craig worked at the construction company. Our relationship felt more friendly than passionate, and passion was one thing I missed in the relationship. But Craig taught me a lot about respecting myself and believing in myself. He was a great partner in business, he protected me, and he taught me invaluable life lessons. The only problem was that he didn't want what I wanted from life.

By this time, I was 27 years old, and I wanted to get married and have a family. Craig didn't like children, which always struck me as ironic since kids were drawn to him. He wanted to focus on his business and wanted nothing to do with starting a family. As a child, Craig lived in poverty, and he would often tell me that his dream was to be rich. He was ashamed of being poor, and growing up, he did his best to hide it the best he could. He hung out with the wealthier students in high school where he met and fell in love with a girl named Robin.

Craig and Robin had been very close, and they often talked about getting married and having a family together. However, none of that came to pass because in his senior year of high school, Robin was killed in a car accident. Craig was still devastated by it when I met him many years later. For the bulk of our relationship, I felt like I was competing for his affections with a ghost. There were certain songs he couldn't listen to, certain foods he'd refuse to eat because it reminded him of Robin and the day she died. Since Robin's death stole his dream of a family from him, Craig vowed he would never get married or have children.

Chapter 6

My First Memory of Law of Attraction

D espite Craig's vow to never marry, our relationship grew into a wonderful friendship. We had some wonderful spiritual people in our life who taught us about meditation and positive thinking. I was hungry for spiritual growth. John and Pam were spiritual counselors who changed my life. Until that point, I had dealt with my past by ignoring it and blocking out the abuse. It had never occurred to me that how I felt about myself and what I attracted was within my control. I felt like a victim. John and Pam became my spiritual parents, the complete set of parents that I'd always wanted. They were wonderful people, and John would host spiritual group seminars on many subjects. John is also the person who taught me how to meditate. I would help out in their office for free counseling lessons. The information there fascinated me, and I'd listen to talks about positive thinking and the Law of Attraction. John, Pam, and the others in the group felt more like a family to me than my own. As an ordained minister, John married Craig and I in a ceremony at their family home. Yes, Craig had a change of heart about marriage. This was a very happy time in my life. Craig and I would enjoy seminars and outings with John and Pam, and every Christmas we'd attend a very special Christmas party hosted by John and Pam. Only a select group of people were invited to the party, and being a part of these special events made me feel so special, happy, and accepted for who I was. It was at these Christmas parties that I was introduced to the Laws of Attraction. Every year, John would ask each of us to write down where we wanted to be the following year. We would then place our secret desires in an envelope and address it to ourselves, and John would mail the sealed envelope back to us just before next year's Christmas party. It was amazing opening the envelope to see what had manifested in my life. One year, I wrote down that I wanted to own a home. The following year, Craig and I bought a newly built home in Issaquah. It was a beautiful home.

When I reflect on these wonderful memories, and the love John and Pam shared with us, my life was easy. I never really wanted for anything. Knowing what I know today, it is when we are living our bliss that our actual life experiences are more aligned with who we are. But at this time, I still didn't fully understand what Law of Attraction was all about. For me, in my limited belief, I could only relate to using the Law of Attraction for manifesting material things. I still wasn't getting the full picture of what it could do for me. Getting married was a small compromise on Craig's part, and I thought it would be enough. Even though I was happy at this stage in my life, I secretly hoped that since Craig had changed his mind on marriage, he would change his mind on having children too. We had many discussions about what we both wanted in life, and it became apparent Craig couldn't or wouldn't give me children. Although we had an overall perfect relationship, we decided it was best to separate.

Chapter 7

Starting Over --- Again

A fter the divorce, I started modeling full-time and doing film work. Although I didn't have a lot of money, I received enough work to support myself financially. My first job, when I was still married to Craig, was a "background" player in the made for TV movie *Jacqueline Bouvier Kennedy*. I played a reporter in one scene. Acting soon became my passion, and I worked as much as I could. I worked for a small production company which sent me out as a set coordinator on several movie sets. I was more fascinated with the production side of film work.

I met Rick only a couple of months after Craig and I divorced. My attraction to Rick was he was the opposite of Craig in terms of his goals. Rick had a stable job, was carefree, and he and his family were a great addition to my life. Looking back on where I was emotionally, I'll admit that I was a bit selfish. At the time, the only thing that mattered to me was having a family, and I take full responsibility for not giving us enough time to really get to know each other. I wanted to get married and start a family as soon as possible. I don't think Rick was ready, but he did want a family and was family-orientated. I also loved how welcoming and accepting his family was of me, especially his mother who I became very close with.

Even though John and Pam didn't live that far away from me, I was not part of their lives anymore. They were still attached to Craig, and when we got divorced, it was hard on them. Thus, I welcomed Rick's family into my heart as my own.

If you haven't noticed yet, my experiences are exactly what I'm attracting emotionally. That's the beauty of Law of Attraction. My life as a child was filled with insecurity, feelings of unworthiness, fear, jealousy and anger. All of my relationships with men brought me exactly what I was emotionally sending out. The world is a mirror of your emotions, and my experiences were a mirror of how I felt. After Rick and I married, life was okay. I started feeling like something was missing, and there was an uneasiness inside me that I couldn't explain. I fought the emotional debate, telling myself I should be happy. After all, I had everything most people want from life, and I finally had the children I always wanted. I had two sons, Christopher and Mark. What could I possible be missing? From 1986 through 1988, I was lucky enough to do more film work. I worked with a Hollywood casting company, White Light Productions. I loved the experiences and the uniqueness of my career, but truthfully, I was emotionally and spiritually dead inside. I had lost all of the emotional highs that I shared with Craig, John, Pam and others. I didn't understand why I felt this way because having a family was so important, but I felt so empty. The only thing that kept me going was working in films, which still brought excitement to me, but at the cost of not being with my two young sons. I finally realized that film work was a band-aid for my depression. I was lost. Empty. Emotionally, there was nothing there. I was very depressed. It felt like I worked hard to nurture my marriage of nearly three years, but maybe I didn't. Rick and I continued to grow apart. I don't think I really even cared about our marriage at this point, and Rick used golf as his emotional bandage. We simply didn't know how to fix our marriage. I missed my mother and sister dearly. I'd not seen them for several years, and I was torn on wanting to return home to be close to them again and feeling obligated to stay in Washington with Rick. Kathy, my former roommate and high school friend, had also moved to Washington and we were reunited. We became close friends again. But even though I had Kathy to share my emotional struggles with, I still felt so very alone.

I finally worked up the courage to do what I knew I had to do. My marriage was over, and I was moving on, searching for what it was I needed to feel whole again. Everyone thought I'd lost my mind when I left, but I knew if I didn't leave, my unhappiness would affect my relationship with my sons and family forever. I was miserable, and I knew I could not continue living like that.

Chapter 8

Starting Over With My Sons

In November 1990, I moved back to Southern California with my sons to start a new life. Now a single mother, I picked myself up to start this new chapter of our lives. Again, that familiar feeling of being free washed over me, and I no longer felt I was trapped in a pit of emotional darkness. I had been searching for life's meaning, wanting to understand more about who I was and what my life purpose might be. Eagerly, I started reading inspirational books and meditated to help me with my search.

But I still did not understand the true meaning of Laws of Attraction. I was still under the impression that it was for material things, and all I had to do was recite affirmations, try to keep positive thoughts, and I'd manifest what I wanted. In fact, I still believed that what I was seeking was material in nature. It wasn't until years later that I realized what I needed, I had. And what I had was really all I needed.

This was a very rough time in my life. Not making enough money to support myself and my sons, I lived paycheck to paycheck. The generosity of my sister, who had a very good job and no children of her own, helped a lot. It was her generosity that put Christmas presents under our tree. I didn't understand why things were so difficult, though. After all, I was emotionally in a good place, what was I doing wrong?

The concept of "believe and have faith" meant I recited affirmations, but I still didn't understand that it needed to be matched with emotion. Most of the books I'd read talked about positive thoughts, but it wasn't until several years later that I read any mentioning adding emotion.

I did not date for about two years after my divorce from Rick. My focus was on raising the boys and trying to figure out what I was going to do next. A very close and dear friend of mine, Bill, told me about a job as a scheduler for an aerial dog fighting company. The company was an entertainment company out of Southern California, and the job made it easier for me to support my sons. I handled marketing, scheduling, and promoting. A family owned business, I was accepted as one of their own. I loved that job because it allowed me to work with people, and the company was unique. It was here that I met Bruce, a retired pilot with the military. Bruce was one of the flight instructors, and we had great chemistry. He wasn't liked by many people because he had a sarcastic demeanor, but he and I got along great. The more we talked, the more we realized we both dreamed of starting our very own aerial dog fighting company.

Chapter 8

A New Move

With two other military pilots as silent partners, Bruce and I moved to a prime location to start our new business in January 1994. This was an exciting time for us. Here I was living in one of the most exciting cities in the world, building a business I loved. I was feeling very blessed because I believed in our business, which was also an aerial combat business, and we met many influential people. Everyone loved the idea, and we had a lot of support to succeed. However, not everything was going so well. Not long after our arrival, Bruce started to show a side of him I'd never really noticed before. He was jealous of the attention I was getting during our promotional meetings. Not only was I more charismatic, I was also persuasive thanks to my movie career. These were traits that Bruce simply didn't have. Many people preferred me over him, including our business attorney and staff. Our two investors couldn't stand to be around him. As business increased, it only seemed to make Bruce's jealousy even worse. People would insist on working only with me. In board meetings, arguments would break out and it was always suggested that we get rid of Bruce. This, of course, put me in a bad position. Everyone from our business attorney, to the silent investors, no one wanted to keep Bruce in the company. It was a challenge bringing in new business as long as he was involved. Ultimately the partners voted him silent, and his duties were limited to that of a flight instructor. Everything else was behind-the-scenes. Prior to starting our business, we'd had one physical confrontation. This should have been a red flag of what was to come, but I took responsibility for the incident, telling myself that Bruce was stressed about the move. I truly believed it was an isolated incident. Here I was in denial once more, focused on an opportunity I wanted very much, and I managed to convince myself that it wouldn't happen again. And this is how I found myself in yet another abusive relationship. However, when this relationship turned abusive, I thought I was the only one being abused. It wasn't until many years later when I started writing this book, that my sons told me Bruce abused them as well. Mark told me Bruce would hold him down with one hand and slap or punch him with the other. Bruce would thump or slap the back of both boys' heads when he walked by them, and both boys avoided being alone with him.

Not knowing about the abuse of my boys, I hid the abuse like before. Or at least, I tried to hide it, but everyone I came into contact with could see the signs. One day, I was meeting with our attorney, Roger, and walked in with a black eye. I attempted to conceal the bruising with makeup, but it wasn't fooling anyone. Roger addressed the issue, and I defended Bruce to the end. I explained that he was under a lot of stress due to issues with the silent partners. The abuse seemed like a small price to pay, and I promised myself that one day I would deal with it. I put my well-being on the back burner in order to succeed. I couldn't fail at this business. I couldn't fail my sons or the other people who believed in me. One Easter while the boys were in Washington with their father, I was in our home office revising a Standard Operating Procedure (SOP) which was to be presented to the FAA the following week. Bruce was watching the *Ten Commandments* as he did every year for Easter, and he asked me to join him. I told him I would as soon as I finished up my work. Twenty minutes later, Bruce came in angry that I hadn't joined him yet. He grabbed me by the hair and dragged me into the family room. I fought back, swinging my arms and kicking, hoping he'd let go. He started kicking me in the sides, then in the head. I couldn't get away from him. I was on the floor and he was standing over me, kicking me over and over again. He tore my clothes off me, dragged me to the front door, pushed me outside and locked me out. It was late in the day, and the sun was setting. I was nearly naked, so I crawled behind the bushes just under the front window where I stayed until it got dark, wondering what I should do. He could see me from the front window, and I spent the next several hours pleading for Bruce to open the door. I felt helpless, desperate, and like I had no control over what was happening to me. It was a horrible feeling. Eventually, Bruce unlocked the door. I would have left if I could, and I knew I would leave as soon as I could, but I simply had no money to do so. Instead, I spent the next several months walking on eggshells, just waiting for it to happen again. There's no worse feeling than that of being trapped and afraid. Later that year, on December 3rd, we hosted a competition for one of the local businesses. One of our airplanes lost control and crashed in the desert just North of the airport, killing both occupants. From the time I listened to the mayday calls over the radio, the entire event was surreal. It felt like watching a movie, it couldn't be real. This tragedy is one the community will never forget. Between the media, the employees, the families of the people killed, the police and coroner, I was on autopilot, moving from one issue after another and after another. I was in a complete state of shock.

On this very same day, another near tragedy hit even closer to home. My boys were being cared for by a babysitter, and she let them go next door to play with a neighbor. Their visiting grandfather locked my oldest son, Chris, in the bathroom and tried to molest him. Chris broke free, and both he and Mark ran home to alert the babysitter.

That day has been, and will always be, the darkest day in my life. The days that followed were filled with the FAA investigation into the crash and the police investigation into the attempted molestation. I felt disconnected, like life had knocked me down and I simply didn't have the strength to pull myself back up again. We had no money, business was down, and I was living in an abusive relationship. I kept thinking it couldn't get any worse than that, and in a strange way, I actually believed I deserved the abuse and all the tragedy surrounding me. I thought I was cursed, and that happiness would never find me. My family still lived in California, and my relationship with my mother was somewhat strained because of Bruce. My mother had finally divorced Bud and was working on her insurance career. My mother was very supportive in the days following the airplane accident, and I learned a lot about settling lawsuits and insurance claims from her. But still, I never told her about the abuse from Bruce.

At this time, my brother was going through a divorce, leaving him a single father with four children. With the help of my mother, they were fighting their own battles. She was helping him with the divorce and the custody issues which ended up going on for years. How could I tell them about the abuse? They had enough on their plate, and I felt like a failure as it was. How could I admit to my family that Bruce was abusing me? Bruce was the reason we were estranged in the first place, and this was simply too much for me to sort out. The investigation of my son's molester ended, the neighbors refused to cooperate with the authorities. They sent their grandfather out of state, and the investigation was closed. The detective told me that the grandfather could never come back into the state of Nevada, and that was all that happened.

As I write about these experiences, it's clear to me that what we believe, we attract. I was no stranger to abuse. The abuse was an imprint of my earlier years, and I was puzzled why I had attracted it back into my life time and time again. I now know that every moment of our lives, we are attracting things to us. We are magnets. What we are focused on and what we are thinking, we are attracting to us. From early on, I felt that my father didn't love me as much as my siblings, and because I didn't feel that he could love me, I developed an inner believe that I was unloveable. This is what I sent out into the world and what came back in my relationships. For a while, I was able to break that abusive energy when I moved to Washington and became involved with John and Pam. During those years I spent with Craig and Rick, there was no abuse. None whatsoever. That's because during that time, I was projecting a more positive self-image. However, that changed when I was with Bruce. I now understand that the relationship was so negative, that it drew even more negative energy to not only my life, but also my boys'. Over the next month, I prayed and started meditating asking for help and direction for my business to be restored so I could move on.

My prayers answered, the investors agreed to purchase another plane and keep the company going. Because of this decision, I felt like I was given another chance. Bruce's abuse once again went on the back burner. This second chance meant the investors believed in me, and even though they didn't want Bruce around the business, they knew how dedicated and passionate I was about making it work. I appreciated their confidence in me, but the conditions to continue were very simple: Bruce could have nothing to do with the company.

This put me in a dangerous position. Bruce was obviously not pleased about this decision. He ended up getting another job, and thankfully, we were able to avoid each other. I worked the business, he worked downtown, making it to where we hardly saw each other. One day at the office, I received a phone call from a woman asking for Bruce. Suspicious, I took a message and headed home where I found him still sleeping. When I asked about the phone call, Bruce laughed and told me she was one of many new women in his life. A few days later, I found a gun. As far as I'd known, Bruce had never owned a gun. I was worried that my relationship with Bruce had taken a dangerous turn, and I was scared for myself and my boys. I took the gun to Roger's office, and Roger called Bruce asking him to move out of our home. He told him then, and only then, he would get the gun back. Bruce moved out without incident, but not before he threatened me. I filed a Temporary Protection Order (TPO) against Bruce, and at the court hearing, the TPO was extended due to statements made by Bruce. That was the last time I ever saw Bruce. A few years later I found out he moved back East somewhere.

Around the same time I was ending my relationship with Bruce, the company experienced a second accident, a mid-air collision, that closed the business indefinitely. Once more, my world was upside down. I was involved in many lawsuits, bankruptcy and other legal proceedings. Since Bruce moved out and I didn't have any income, I was forced to break the lease on the home we were living in and rent the cheapest house available. I was emotionally drained at this point, and I felt so defeated. I was ashamed, and I felt like a complete failure. The house I rented was run down and infested with cockroaches. The morning after we moved in, I got the boys ready for school, and we headed out the front door to find my car was no longer in the driveway. It had been repossessed.

Chapter 9

Police Academy

The next two years were a struggle for me both financially and emotionally. I knew I needed to make some serious changes. But change was a slow process for me. I had the inner drive to not only survive, but to be successful. I knew that my life could change, I just wasn't quite sure how to go about making it happen. I wanted stability in not only my life, but my sons' lives as well.

I decided to get back into law enforcement. I spent the next two years testing for the local police departments, finally securing a job at one of the detention centers as an inmate records clerk. This was far from the position I wanted, but I had been placed on the Police Officer and Correction Officer availability list, so it was a start.

I also vowed to myself, for the sake of my sons, that I would not enter into another relationship without understanding why my relationships turned abusive. I worried that not having a positive role model in my father, and losing him when I was young, had damaged me in a way I wasn't sure I could fix. I often wondered if he had lived, would things have been different? I worked in the detention center until 2001 when I entered the police academy. I'd always planned on becoming a police officer after graduating college, and my hard work and discipline was finally paying off, or so I thought. The academy was brutal, however, and it was a challenge for me to keep up. At 46 years old, I was in the minority, a woman and the second oldest person in the academy. It was approximately eighteen weeks of intense physical training and learning the law and procedures. The physical side was the most challenging for me. We had formation runs several times a week for miles, and the state required agility which tested your strength and endurance.

Before going into the academy, I thought I understood how hard it would be. I believed with my past, I could handle anything. I thought there was no limit to what I could do. However, my instructors didn't have the same confidence in me that I had within myself. They didn't think I could pass. I was told that the first week, when they asked me if I would consider dropping out to go back to the detention center. I was singled out by my instructors, and they leaned on me with no mercy. They would make me run laps around the parking lot or do pushups while everyone else was taking their hourly break. Three times a week, this was followed by a formation run. Often, another recruit was assigned to watch me, which meant that recruit didn't get their break. This obviously created resentment, and slowly, it separated me from them. I was exhausted.

On top of the constant physical demands, there was the daily assigned homework which prevented me from getting much sleep. Many nights, in addition to the homework, I was assigned essays. One week, I was assigned two 1,000 word essays, a 250 word essay, and two 5,000 word essays. That week, I wrote over 12,000 words in addition to everything else that they had me to do.

The instructor was trying hard to break me, but I fought back even harder. I wasn't going to give up. I couldn't fail again.

I made it into my third month, but experienced trouble qualifying with my firearm. Before I went into the academy, I purchased my own firearm. Not knowing much about them, the gun I bought was too heavy and too large for my hands. We were required to put thirty-six rounds in the center of the target, and consistently, I would get thirty-five rounds in, dropping the last round just out of the target. It was clear that my firearm was too heavy. I thought maybe I'd get some help, or at least get to change out my gun. At the end of qualification week, I was assigned to work with the range master over the weekend. He assured me I didn't have a problem, and I would get used to the gun. "Just practice," he told me.

The following Monday, I felt confident I would qualify when retested. I was taken out with two other recruits to re-qualify. Again, thirty-five were within the target perimeter, and just one below the line. It was when I returned to the academy to find my training books and gear sitting on the counter that I realized I was being dropped from the academy. I was told to walk to my car and not return. The department would be contacting me with further instruction. The next day, I was non-confirmed as a police officer. I was turned down. I was devastated as I knew in my heart that this was where I was supposed to be.

The news came just before Christmas, and I was unemployed. As if things couldn't get much worse, during a physical exam, a small lump had been found in my right breast and I was still waiting for the test results. Once again, I was at the lowest point in my life. I felt like I had nowhere to go or anyone to turn to for emotional support. My mother had passed away a couple of years before, and my sister and brother were living their own lives. I had no one. On Christmas Eve, at the insistence of my brother and sister, we headed to my brother's house for Christmas. I knew my devastation was affecting Chris and Mark, and I wanted them to be with family. While playing with his cousin's, Chris was riding a scooter and stepped down with his left foot to stop. He landed wrong, and ended up breaking his ankle in seven places. My sister and I spent Christmas Eve in the emergency room with Chris, and to make things even more complicated, I didn't have insurance. The doctor said he needed surgery, but without health insurance, they refused to treat him. They released him later that night, and we took him back to my brother's to sleep. My brother's house was so small, my sister and I had to stay in a motel down the street.

On Christmas day, we headed back home with Chris stretched out in the backseat of our car. At fifteen, he was nearly six foot three, and it was hard for him to get comfortable during the five-hour trip home. When we got back, we found out that Chris was covered under his father's insurance and he was able to see a specialist receiving his surgery a few weeks later.

Chapter 10

My Career

In January 2002, a Community Service Officer (CSO) position opened up. I tested with 150 other applicants, and I got the job. At this time, I was still very depressed and my coping mechanisms consisted of prayer and meditation. I wasn't sure what my religious beliefs were, but I knew there was something there, somewhere. Although some days, I didn't think I'd make it, I always had this feeling or sense of knowing that I would be okay.

I enjoyed working as a CSO, but it wasn't what I wanted to do. When I was rehired, I went into field training the same time my academy graduated. We were all together in the six weeks of the post-academy. The wounds were still fresh from failing out of the academy, and now I endured humiliation from my peers. To add to my tension, my first assigned field-training officer was one of my instructors from the academy. He didn't like me then, and he certainly didn't like me now. I could only suck it up and make sure I passed my field training.

Field training last about four months, and although my next set of training officers were great, I had to start thinking about where my career was going. A new Chief of Police came to the department and after hearing about my experience, wanted to put me back through the academy, but that never happened. I worked as a CSO for three years, and during that time, I took online courses preparing to test for the position of Crime Scene Investigator (CSI). I studied hard and on scenes where both myself and the CSI responded, I asked questions and watched them process the scene. The first time I tested for CSI, I failed, but I didn't give up. I tried again the following year, in 2005, and this time I passed. In April 2005, I joined the Crime Scene Unit. Working as a CSI has been a privilege and an honor, and there isn't a single day that I'm not grateful. Dealing with the types of calls we have, and coping with this career is not for the light-hearted, by any means, but I sincerely believe I'm in this position for a reason. Not only that, but my life's experience has prepared me for this position. Why? I can't entirely say, but I know one thing: I have survived through many traumatic experiences. I've had my highs, and I've had my lows, and sometimes I wasn't sure I could ever dig my way out. But all of these things have made me the person I am today. Not only am I strong, but I have compassion and a positive attitude. Daily, I see horrendous crimes, people suffering, and I'm surrounded by death. I've come to understand society as a whole. I've paid attention to how people treat one another, I've seen what poverty does to some, but not others. I understand that sometimes the rich believe an entirely different set of rules that apply only to them. The men and women that work by my side, including the report writers, police officers, evidence techs and detectives, we all share a unique thread in this life. The respect we have for one another is something I'll remember for the rest of my life.

Don't get me wrong, this isn't an easy career to work in. But this position has given me the privilege to witness so much, and I continue to grow spiritually. Even though I believe with all my heart that we can change our lives and create the life we want, I also know that some people will never understand that they have a choice.

I continued reading books from inspiration authors in my search for finding my life's purpose. Although my life started to calm down, I still experienced some highs and lows. The year I became a CSI was a very positive year, and in addition to the new career, I was able to buy a beautiful home. However, in 2008, I lost that home to foreclosure. The experience was painful as this was my dream home, and I felt that I had failed my faith in the Law of Attraction. I believed through so many Law of Attraction books I read, the simple idea of keeping a positive outlook, saying positive affirmations, and meditating was all I needed to do to manifest what I wanted in life and I was suppose to do this no matter what was happening in my life at the time.

I also watched *The Secret Behind the Secret* and the concept of *feeling* along with believing became clear to me. It wasn't enough to stand in front of the mirror and recite affirmations or meditate for the perfect outcome, there was more to it than that. It wasn't until I recognized that it goes beyond what you say to yourself consciously, it needs to become part of your subconscious as well. Losing my home proved that I still had more to learn, and it wasn't until later I learned about combining energy and vibrations with feelings as the fuel. I'll explain more about that in the coming chapters.

Chapter 11

Universal Laws

Though we are taught at an early age that there are laws governing gravity, time, and space, those are actually not Universal laws. Those are agreements in this physical dimension, though other dimensions do exist that do not share those same agreements.

There are in fact, three Universal laws. The Universal Law of Attraction; The Deliberate Law of Creation; and The Art of Allowing. These are the only Universal Laws.

The first is law, the Law of Attraction puts forth that which is like unto itself, is drawn. The Law of Attraction affects all things, and there is nothing that exists that is unaffected by it.

The second law, the Law of Deliberate Creation states that what you give thought to, believe and expect, is then created.

The third law, the Art of Allowing, that I am that which I am, and I am willing to allow all others to be that which they are. Basically, when you accept others and are willing to allow others to be who and what they are, it is only then you are open and begin manifesting your dreams and desires.

Understanding these three powerful Universal Laws and then deliberately applying them to your life will lead you to a joyous state of creating your own life experiences exactly as you want them to be. Every experience occurs because you're inviting it through your thoughts, beliefs, or observation. It's not other people creating these experiences for you, it's all within your control. You are your own creator; that's the law.

Because the Law of Attraction responds to your thoughts and your desires, the evidence of what you are bringing into your life will become apparent. Attraction applies to all things in your life – those things that are wanted, as well as those that are not. It is important to understand that whenever you think of something from the past, the present or perhaps something in the future, you are releasing a vibration into the Universe. The Universe will then match that vibration and send all things, people and experiences back to you. I can't stress it enough that when I say that the Law of Attraction is responding to you, it really is responding to you.

One analogy that might make understanding the Law of Attraction, is to think of it as a magnet. We've all used magnets and understand the basic principles of them – when you place a magnet next to a lunchbox, paperclip, staples, or another metal item, the magnet will pull that metal toward it. When considering the Law of Attraction, and applying that analogy to your own life, if you are feeling down or depressed, you cannot draw happy or joyful events and people to you. Likewise, if you feel, or believe yourself to be poor, you will not be able to attract prosperity to yourself.

To put it simply, when you see or feel something that you like and give attention to it through your thoughts, you are attracting it to you. On the flip side though, the same goes for seeing or feeling something you don't like. By giving it thought, you are still drawing it to you. In this attraction-based Universe, there is no such thing as exclusion from what you do want or what you don't want. The Universe simply responds to the energies generated by thought.

Once you understand this Law, you will understand that by watching the news on television, or seeing a violent movie, or perhaps by merely observing somebody else's difficult experience, you are giving energy through thought to what you are seeing. You are thereby drawing attention to those negative things and are ultimately attracting them into your life. Once you understand this basic principle, I believe you will understand how easy it is to attract those negative things into your life, which should make it easier for you to focus on the things that will attract happy and joyful experiences to yourself.

I've often wondered how I can share an experience with someone that is surrounded by drama and negativity without attracting it to myself. For example, at work, if there is a co-worker you can't quite get along with, or a family member that you choose not to be around, how can you share your experiences without drawing the negativity into your own life? Sometimes, the solution isn't as simple as not being around those types of people or situations.

In cases such as those, I've found that focusing on the third Law, The Art of Allowing, helps put it in perspective and offers some real explanations. For me, accepting that person or circumstance for what it is and who they are, while keeping my own balance, my own joy with who I am, no matter what they are doing, is keeping me in an allowing state. You can choose to simply not focus on the negative aspects of it all, and allow yourself to remain focused on the positive. If you really look for it, there is always something positive you can find within a person, and by choosing to focus on the positive, the negative aspects of the situation will fade away. If you are not inviting it into your life, it cannot stay in your experience.

By being aware of the Law of Attraction, and by staying focused on a subject of your choosing, your point of attraction will become much more powerful. There is power in focusing. As you come to realize that whatever you are giving your attention to is getting larger, you will become more conscious about those things that you choose to give you attention to. It is much easier to change the direction of a thought in the early stages; than it is when that thought has manifested into something you don't want.

Chapter 12

Law of Attraction

Have you ever noticed that sometimes things somehow magically fall into place that allow you to attain something you really wanted? Or maybe you have a thought about calling someone you haven't spoken to in a while, and they call you out of the blue? Or perhaps you notice that there is a negative situation or relationship that keeps appearing and weaving itself throughout your life? Is it happenstance? Serendipity? Just a coincidence? Many of us believe that there are no happy coincidences or cases of happenstance. It's called the Law of Attraction.

The Law of Attraction is not about wishing for love, money, or success to fall into your life. It's nothing that easy. And it's not just about reciting positive affirmations. My hope is, that by the end of this book, you will understand what I mean when I talk about the Law of Attraction and what it can do for you.

What is the Law of Attraction? It's simple. What we think about and what we feel, is drawn to us. In that vibration we send out, the Universe matches it, and sends it back to us with situations and circumstances that match the vibration we sent out to begin with. If we send out positive energy, we receive positive energy. If we send out negative energy, we get the same in return. The Universe is impartial and doesn't know good or bad. The Universe gives you exactly what you ask for through the vibrations you send out. You are a living magnet; you attract people, situations and circumstances into your life that are in direct harmony with your thoughts.

The Law of Attraction the most powerful Law in the Universe, and everybody you know, everybody in your life is affected by it in one way or another. Most without even realizing it. It is the basis of everything we manifest. It's important to understand it, and the power of it before you can fully take control of manifesting the life you want.

What I have learned is that *everything* in the Universe is measured as a vibration and everything is energy. People have energy and vibrations, animals have energy and vibrations, even our buildings and material things have an energy and vibration of their own. You are a magnet and when you send out a vibration, the Universe matches it and sends it back to you in kind.

Despite what some might think, simply speaking about positive things isn't enough either. You must embody the feeling and *feel* the emotion of what you desire as if you already have it. At the beginning of this book there is chart, The Emotional Scale which lists the range of emotions that bring your higher vibrations. The emotions with the highest vibrations are perhaps unsurprisingly, joy, appreciation and love. Consciously allowing yourself to experience these things in your life, or allowing yourself to exist more in the moment, can also raise your emotional vibrations. Each day, through meditation, and prayer, I would raise my self-awareness to a higher vibration. And by connecting my vibration to my desires with the affirmations, the Universe matched them.

Looking back at my past abusive relationships, I existed in a constant state of fear and negativity. I was focused on *not* wanting any more abuse, but the fact that I was *focused* on the abuse is what brought more of it into my life. The Universe simply matched my thoughts. It doesn't understand that I did *not* want it, it just responded to the feeling I had when I was thinking about the abuse. And thinking about the abuse lowered my vibration to fear, depression, despair – all of the emotions that are at the bottom of The Emotional Scale. In many of my abusive relationships, I kept it a secret from people. But I couldn't hide the abuse or the negative vibrations from the Universe. It was because of this cycle that I continued to attract the people and circumstances that matched that vibration, the vibration of abuse.

The Law of Attraction is a wonderful thing to understand. Because of it, for once in my adult life, I know I can change my surroundings or situations.

EMOTIONS

Your emotions are your physical indication of your relationship with who you are and your guidance mechanism of what is wanted or unwanted in your life.

To make this more clear, imagine something that happened in your experience that left you in a bad place emotionally – whether what happened was because of a conscious choice you made or was because you weren't more deliberate about what you wanted. The negative feeling inside of you is your indication that what happened is not in alignment with who you are or perhaps with your inner self.

On the other hand, when you experience something that gives you joy and allows you to feel appreciation, love, and excitement, you are closer to being in alignment with who you are. To make it easier to live a life based on the Law of Attraction, simply pay attention to how you're feeling rather than try to monitor your every thought.

Chapter 13

Energy/Vibration

W e are taught to believe only what we can see and touch. And we're never taught to recognize what our thoughts, emotions and body are telling us. We're never taught about emotional energy or Universal vibrations. Everything around us is vibrating. In fact, we each have our own vibration, and that vibration is what we send out to the universe. Awakening to this way of thinking, and understanding this new way of looking at yourself will transform your life as it has mine, and so many others.

We start with a thought, and that thought is connected to a feeling. It is the feeling and thought that sends out a vibration, and vibration is what the Law of Attraction sends back to you and into your life, wanted or not. You have the power within yourself to choose what you think about, to choose how you feel, and change your vibration.

In society today, the vast majority of the general population is consumed with low vibrational thought. War, poverty, crime, fear, stress, and other negative thoughts occupy our minds. We are fed low vibrational information through the media and left feeling bad, scared, and fearful. You watch the ten o'clock newscast and go to bed with the negative feelings it inspires within you. You fall asleep feeling these negative emotions, having these low vibrational thoughts, and when you awake, you awake with the same vibration. We then walk through life in low vibration, attracting unpleasant and unwanted things that will match it, caught in a negative loop without even realizing it.

As I mentioned before, the example of waking up with a low vibration means that your morning is going less well then you'd want. Maybe your alarm didn't go off, or an unexpected situation came up causing you to be late for work. You arrive at work complaining about what happened and you are still putting out the negative vibration, so now the momentum of negativity is building, as are the unpleasant experiences you are now receiving during your day. By the time you clock out and go home, you are completely disgusted and frustrated with the day's events. And all of the day's frustrations and negativity has been of your own creation. I say that because you allowed yourself to focus your attention – and energy – on the negative information you were receiving from the news or from whatever negative situation came up. You defaulted to the same negative emotions in the morning that you'd had when you went to bed the night before and allowed your focus and energy to remain there. You can control how your days will unfold by allowing yourself to go to sleep feeling positive and uplifted. Do that and the chances are very good that is exactly how you will wake up.

Vibrations have been confirmed by many an author and I continually find added confirmation as I explore the different teachings by different people. Because of what I have learned and experienced myself, I have come to believe with my entire heart and soul is that one's life experience is directly influenced by our emotional vibrations and that raising those vibrations to a state of joy and happiness is one of life's very simple secrets to manifesting your life the way you want it to be.

A study on vibration by Dr. David Hawkins calibrated energy and emotions on a "Scale of Consciousness"

On Hawkins' scale, you can see that Enlightment is scored at 700, Joy at 540 and Love at 500. The average level of humanity right now is Apathy, which is 207. The study also shows the current vibrational level by country. The Middle East is at 170, China at 300, India at 355, and the USA at 421. In our society, we are brought up by parents telling us how we should act, based on how they believe we should behave. Their attempt to force us to conform to their behavioral ideals often includes guilt and shame, manipulation. Most of us will still carry the shame and guilt throughout our adult lives. In other words, because of experiences in our childhoods, we go through life vibrating at a low 20 or 40, doing the best we can to dodge life's experiences.

When I started studying vibration, I found it fascinating. I began to understand why my past experiences happened to me – and why they continued to happen to me into adulthood. I then had to find the courage to accept and take responsibility for these experiences. I was no victim; I was the creator of them and that was a big pill to swallow.

The change starts with you. With the decision you must make to change. I had to take responsibility for everything that happened to me. EVERYTHING! I then had to forgive myself before I could forgive anyone else. And I was able to do that. I was able to forgive everyone in my past. Forgiveness is one of the tools we must master in order to release the negative emotions that keep you in low vibration. It is a necessary tool and one technique I used was Emotional Frequency Techniques (EFT), better-known as "Tapping".

Chapter 14

Meditation

Meditation is nothing more than having a quiet mind, being able to draw your consciousness within and being in the moment. There is nothing complex about it, but it does take a lot practice to quiet your mind. There is no time limit you must do, or any particular time of day. It's all up to you. For me, the quiet outside world of the early morning or late night helps me quiet my mind. Meditation is connecting to your inner self, to your truth. Many times when I am in the moment, with a quiet mind, I invite God, my guide, and the angels to surround me, to connect with me. Sometimes I choose to meditate to music or to a mantra. There is no right or wrong way to meditate. It's all in what feels right to you and the best technique is the one that fits you.

My techniques have changed over the years, but I would always choose to start my day with some meditation. I spend a few moments giving gratitude for a wonderful night of sleep and gratitude for whatever else comes to mind. I'd send blessings of love and light to my family, my co-workers, neighbors, close friends, and anyone else

I felt compelled to send them to, and at the end of my ritual, I always sent blessings to my guides, angels and to the Universe.

If I am not pressed for time, I spend a couple of minutes visualizing myself holding my Blessing Ball of Light for Today and in it I imagine placing everything I want or need for the day. After I'm finished, I visualize bringing the Blessing Ball into my heart repeating "I bless myself with love and light, I bless myself with source energy." By the time my feet hit the ground to start my day, I have elevated my vibration to a wonderful state and I was ready for whatever life threw at me. This exercise I got from Christy Sheldon, and is one I still enjoy using.

Chapter 17

Positive Affirmations and Self Talk

A great many Law of Attraction books will talk about affirmations. Self-talk is probably challenging to most people as it is that little voice in your head, the same voice that swears out your boss, and cusses at a driver who cut you off. It's that little voice that tells you its too early to get up, and that you hate going to work. I think of anything that is important you come to understand is being conscious of the self-talk. We all do it. From waking up in the morning, all throughout the day, and when we close our eyes at night.

Have you ever woken up on the wrong side of the bed feeling grumpy? Maybe you had to get up and go to a job you hated and it made you deeply unhappy. This is your first vibrational feeling and it has set the tone for your entire day. Here's the scenario: You probably got up, stubbed your toe, AND you were running late. You jump in the shower and because you're already running late, you're in such a hurry, you flip the faucet with such force that it spits out hot, hot water, making you scream because you burned yourself. After your shower, you go downstairs and the coffee pot won't work. Now you're running even further behind and as a result, you're really frustrated and angry. Your self-talk is "Why Me?" And your mantra becomes "I hate mornings." Off you go to work with a very low vibration which, even without your knowing, will make your unpleasant experiences continue throughout the day.

A little challenge I like to give people is this: before closing your eyes at night, think of something perfect, beautiful, or something that brings joy into your life. In the morning, just before you open your eyes, be mindful of that feeling you thought the night before. It is that feeling you need to come back to. In other words, if you fall asleep angry, you will wake up angry. But if you fall asleep with something perfect and joyful in mind, you will wake up that was as well.

What I have learned over the years, mostly by experience, is that we have control over how we feel, and ultimately what type of day we will have. Our life experiences are based on emotion, vibration, and the manifestation of what we bring into our lives. If there is only one thing I hope you get out of this book, it is this: You have a choice.

Chapter 18

Forgiveness

Forgiveness comes from the heart unconditionally;
Or it doesn't come at all

The importance of forgiveness is more crucial than you realize. It's also the hardest thing to do. Forgive yourself. Unless we can forgive ourselves, we can never hope to forgive someone else. Forgiving yourself for any situation is taking responsibility for your part. It's not, as some people thing, being a victim, and it is learning whatever you can from that experience.

To forgive someone who has hurt us can be almost unthinkable. I understand that, and I have been there. Most of us need someone to blame for our shortcomings, or the bad things that happen in our lives, and to not forgive someone, to hold on to that anger and resentment, showcases that perfectly. If we forgive, we also need to take responsibility for our part in the situation. If someone has hurt you emotionally, then you need to take responsibility for allowing yourself to be hurt. To forgive is the single most defining action you can take toward changing your vibrations and thus, changing your life. Most of us feel we have power over someone when we don't forgive, but it is actually the exact opposite. To carry resentment, anger, hate, jealousy, guilt and shame is giving *them* the power over you.

> *To forgive is to set a prisoner free and*
> *discover that prisoner was you.*
> ~ Lewis B. Smedes

Let's spend a moment looking at forgiveness. If you think about someone you cannot or will not forgive, how does that make you feel? Does it inspire anger? Fear? Resentment? Holding on to all of that and not allowing yourself to forgive is definitely a lower vibration. This is the part where you can make a major shift in your vibration by forgiving and letting go. Ask yourself right now, what benefit is not forgiving someone doing for you? If you are holding on to all of those negative emotions, you are hurting only yourself.

Most of us carry around our anger, resentment, and jealousy. Most of us carry some negative emotion directed toward others, even those people no longer in our lives. You must understand that these negative emotions affect the quality of your life and the lives of those around you. It's hard to experience love, compassion, joy and happiness, if you are a prisoner of your own negative emotions. When you hold resentment and cannot forgive somebody that has wronged you, you are binding yourself to that person. Forgiveness is the act of unchaining yourself from the thoughts and feelings that bind you to that person or situation. Forgiveness is the only way to release yourself from those bonds.

Forgiveness is a creative act; it transforms us from prisoners of the past to liberators of the present, as we step into the future.

When we forgive, we release the control and power that person has over us and we stop allowing ourselves to play the victim. We no longer define ourselves by how we have been hurt, but instead by how we have grown. Life either expands or contracts in direct proportion to the courage it takes to forgive. Forgiveness has two parts: The lesser is to forgive others, the greater is to forgive you. And it is the single most important process that brings peace and harmony to our lives.

To err is human, to forgive divine.
~ Alexander Pope -

Chapter 19

Putting It All Together

I started this book by sharing a glimpse of my life and the challenges I've experienced. I did this because I wanted you, the reader, to understand that I had many obstacles and challenges, and that nothing really came easy for me. Not until I understood the Law of Attraction, forgiveness, and expanded my spiritual understanding.

My relationships with Bud, Jack, and Bruce were abusive. But relationships I experienced and enjoyed after them were not. Now that I understand the concept that what you think about and what you feel is what you attract, my life has brought me to a place where I am enjoying a great career and a circle of loving friends and family. My past experiences showed me what I didn't want, which birthed an understanding of what I did want. And though it was difficult in the moment, I look back upon it now knowing that I wouldn't change a thing.

So my journey continues. This book may be written but I continue to experience the wonderful lessons that my journey provides me. My life is full of miracles and I continue to serve myself with self-love and honor, as I serve others. The best part is that I still have so much more to learn.

I am hopeful that something in this book will inspire you to get excited about your own journey and your own truth. Embrace yourself with love and stake your claim to your birthright of abundance.

In your journey of self-discovery, explore the different avenues to answer the questions that you need to be answered. I did a lot of my research online. Also, it is vital to trust in who you are at this moment and to stop second-guessing your intuition. Once you allow yourself to grow comfortable trusting your own intuition, your life will become so much easier. Stop listening to the judgment of others. Stop letting them tell you what you should and shouldn't do. Your life's journey is about you and your experiences. This isn't being selfish, it is about respecting and loving yourself. The difference? A selfish act is perpetrated against another, meant to benefit only you. Self-love is performing an act that brings you closer to alignment with who you are.

Start waking up feeling like it is Christmas morning, and taking the time to put intention into how you want your day to go. At night, just before you fall asleep, give gratitude and appreciation for everything that happened that day. Even if there was something unpleasant that happened, give gratitude for the experience and ask for the meaning, for what you are meant to learn from it.

Mentally love and bless everyone throughout the day. Especially those you don't care for. And lastly, please *please* take the time to forgive. Forgive *everyone,* especially yourself, and give gratitude for the experience.

Chapter 20

Start Your Journey

W hen I started reading about the Law of Attraction, I read books authored by Dwayne Dyer, as well as Esther and Jerry Hicks. Most notably, I read *Ask and It is Given*; *Law of Attraction*, and *The Secret,* which was written by Rhonda Byrnes, with consultation by Esther and Jerry Hicks. I was hooked and was hungry to learn more. I thoroughly enjoyed the teachings and seminars given by Esther and Jerry Hicks, perhaps better known as Abraham-Hicks and will always be thankful for their dedication and work. It wasn't until I watched *"The Secret Behind The Secret",* featuring Ester and Jerry Hicks, that I finally started to understand the concept of emotions and vibration. It was then that I fully understood that every person, animal, and thing have their own vibration, and that what was attracted depended upon the level of the vibration.

My favorite books to read are listed on the next page. Those are just a few of the authors that helped expand my awareness, but certainly not all. There are many authors out there and it really just comes down to who you connect with. It's that simple.

Don't worry about which book to start reading. Just pick one up and see if it resonates with you. You'll just have to trust me when I say that the books that are important for you to read, you will pick. I started out reading books by Louise Hay and then moved on to the many books by Abraham-Hicks. Somewhere in that time I picked up a book titled, *Manifest Your Destiny*, by Dr. Wayne Dyer. After purchasing his book, I placed this book on the book shelf and it sat there unread for at least two years. One day when I was looking at the books in my bookshelf, *"Manifest Your Destiny"* caught my eye and I realized that I had never read it. I sat down and read it from cover to cover. I couldn't put it down. For me, this is yet another example of receiving information when the time is right and the exact time when you need it. Trust in the timing of things.

When you are ready to do some healing, Margaret Lynch has several wonderful programs to assist you in clearing out old beliefs, or blocks. For me, clearing was a way for me to release the past guilt, shame and anger that I'd carried around for so long.

> "The best and most beautiful things
> in the world cannot be seen or
> Even touched – they must be felt with the heart"
> Helen Keller

Reference of Books

These are just some of the books that have helped me:

By Louise Hay
You Can Heal Your Life

By Iyanla Vanzant
One Day My Soul Just Opened Up: 40 days and 40 Nights Toward Spiritual Strength and Personal Growth,
In the Meantime: Finding Yourself and the Love You Want,
Yesterday
I Cried: Celebrating the Lessons of Living and Loving.

Esther and Jerry Hicks
Ask and It is Given
Law of Attraction
The Amazing Power of Deliberate Intention
The Vortex
Getting Into The Vortex
Money and The Law of Attraction
The Sarah Books (1,2,3)

DWAYNE DYER
Change Your Thoughts, Change Your Life
Manifest Your Destiny
Don't Die With Your Music Still in You (with Serena J. Dyer)

RHONDA BYRNE
The Secret
The Power
The Magic

JACK CANFIELD
The Chicken Soup (series)
The Success Principles
And many, many more......

Tapping into Ultimate Success